English Homework for Key Stage 2

The *Active Homework* series is a unique collection of practical worksheets, providing 'pencil-free', hands-on activities for English, maths and science, which teachers can use as extension activities in the classroom, or give to pupils as homework to do with members of their family or friends. Practical tasks and discussions form the basis for effective learning, with children and their families learning together.

Each book in the series contains practical activities, utilising everyday resources, which align with the National Curriculum, and the relevant National Strategy documents or QCA schemes of work.

Also Available:

Science Homework for Key Stage 2

Colin Forster, Vicki Parfitt, Andrea McGowan and illustrated by David Brookes

Forthcoming:

Maths Homework for Key Stage 2

Vicki Parfitt, Colin Forster, Andrea McGowan and illustrated by David Brookes

English Homework for Key Stage 2

Activity-based learning

Andrea McGowan,
Colin Forster and Vicki Parfitt

Illustrated by David Brookes

First published 2010
by Routledge
2 Park Square, Milton Park, Abingdon, Oxon OX14 4RN

Simultaneously published in the USA and Canada
by Routledge
270 Madison Ave, New York, NY 10016

Routledge is an imprint of the Taylor & Francis Group, an informa business

Typeset in Frutiger by Wearset Ltd, Boldon, Tyne and Wear
Printed and bound in Great Britain by MPG Books Group, UK

British Library Cataloguing in Publication Data
A catalogue record for this book is available from the British Library

Library of Congress Cataloging in Publication Data
McGowan, Andrea.
English homework for key stage 2: activity-based learning/Andrea McGowan, Colin Forster and Vicki Parfitt, illustrated by David Brookes.
    p. cm.
   1. English language – Study and teaching (Elementary) – Activity programs – Great Britain. 2. Homework – Great Britain.
3. Education, Elementary – Parent participation – Great Britain.
4. Active learning – Great Britain. I. Forster, Colin. II. Parfitt, Vicki. III. Title.
   LB1576.M3978 2010
372.60941 – dc22   2009015900

ISBN10: 0-415-47455-8 (pbk)
ISBN10: 0-203-86775-0 (ebk)

ISBN13: 978-0-415-47455-9 (pbk)
ISBN13: 978-0-203-86775-4 (ebk)

To GB.
Thank you.

Contents

Reading and responding

Spelling, punctuation and structure

Guidance for the teacher: how to use this 'pencil-free' homework book

Introduction

Many primary school teachers feel frustrated when they find themselves setting homework that they know isn't helping the children with their learning. Maybe the tasks are boring, poorly matched to the children's abilities, and too worksheet oriented. Maybe they know the tasks do nothing to reinforce learning, but instead reinforce negative feelings about learning. Many teachers feel frustrated that setting, collecting and marking homework is a chore with little return in terms of children's learning. Too often homework can become a site of tension between teachers and children and between teachers and parents, not to mention between children and parents, and the home–school partnership is diminished, not strengthened.

English Homework for Key Stage 2 is a resource that aims to make homework a more positive experience for all concerned, especially children.

Pedagogy and philosophy

Primary school teachers know that children learn through doing and that talking about their experiences is a crucial part of the learning process, as it enables children to revisit and reinforce ideas by reworking them in their own words. However, for many children, homework has become synonymous with 'doing the worksheet' and for many parents homework is about 'getting the sheet done'.

English Homework for Key Stage 2 provides good opportunities for learning through doing and for parents/carers to talk with their children about their ideas. *English Homework for Key Stage 2* enables teachers to set homework that they feel is learning-focused, rather than task-focused, and helps foster positive relationships between all members of the school community.

English Homework for Key Stage 2: the key ideas

- *English Homework for Key Stage 2* is pencil-free; the homework sheets are not worksheets – there is nothing for the child to 'fill in'.
- Parents and carers are encouraged to share the homework with the child through activity and discussion (but it doesn't just have to be parents – it could be anyone in the family or household).

- The activities are done with items and materials found in the home and focus on discussion.
- Since there is nothing for the child to fill in on the sheet, there is nothing for the teacher to collect and mark, but there will be lots to talk about in a follow-up discussion.
- The homework is arranged in strands to correspond to the new PNS Framework for Literacy.
- There is a blank template for teachers to use to devise their own homework activities to allow for further creativity and development.

Following-up on the homework

Whether you select a homework that follows up on work done in class or that introduces a new idea, it is important to follow it up with a class-based discussion about the homework. It would be valuable to find out how the children got on, what they learnt, whether their parents or carers learnt anything and if they raised any good questions about the topic. In this way, it is clear that homework is not a stand-alone activity, but part of a learning process that combines both home and school experiences.

Possible follow-up activities

- Class discussion, with the children reporting on how they got on and what they found out.
- Class discussion, with the children sharing any questions they raised while doing the activities.
- Group discussions, with each group deciding the most important things they found out.
- Group discussions, with each group deciding which is their favourite question from the ones they all raised.
- Group presentation based on their homework.

Partnership with parents

It is important to keep parents informed of the purpose of the homework and their role in their children's learning. We have provided a draft letter that might be used each term to remind them of the approach taken in *English Homework for Key Stage 2*. You may like to use a home–school book for parents to provide some feedback on how they and their children got on with the homework.

Template letter

Dear Parent/Carer

English homework

Our new English topic this term is _____ and we will be exploring the following ideas:

-

-

-

The English homework we will be giving on this topic will aim to reinforce these ideas through **doing** and **talking**; we will not be asking the children to fill in a worksheet for their homework as we don't believe that this will help them learn.

Why doing and talking? Children learn much more by telling other people about their understanding than they do by being 'told' stuff, and doing active tasks gives them lots to talk about and experiences to reflect on.

It's not just good for children: Parents and carers often don't get to hear much from their children about what they're doing at school, and sharing a discussion is a good way in to finding out how much your children are learning.

Another advantage: Homework can sometimes become a battleground; we hope children will need less nagging to do this homework and that they, and you, will learn a lot from doing it and possibly even enjoy some of it.

Feedback to the school: If you want to, you can write feedback on the homework sheet so that staff back at school know how your child got on with the homework. It would be useful for the school to know if your child grasped the ideas well or explained them clearly or if they learnt anything from doing the activities. You might also give some feedback on whether they enjoyed the tasks.

How the school will follow up the homework: Your child's teacher will organise a time for the children to discuss and share their experience of doing the activities. This will give the children the chance to reinforce their learning and for the teacher to assess their progress.

Blank active homework template

Aim of the activity

-
-
-

Think about and discuss

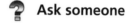 **Ask someone**

 **Tell someone**

Speaking, listening and interacting

Be a performer

Look at the short poem below and think about how you could 'perform' it so that it's really engaging for your listeners.

Try and learn it off by heart and practise sharing the poem.

Storm
The lightning flashes split the sky
As thunder rolled round,
The rain drops fell from clouds up high
And thumped upon the ground.
The air was heavy, dark and cold
As creatures ran for cover,
But just as brightening skies foretold
The storm has now passed over.

Think about and discuss

What makes a really good, entertaining performance?

What kind of expression works best for this text?

How would you perform your favourite poem or verse from a book?

Love fifteen

Prepare to play 'word tennis' with a partner. Toss a coin to decide who goes first.

Player 1 starts with 'big' and puts it in a sentence, e.g. the elephant was wearing really *big* boots.

Without hesitating, Player 2 suggests an alternative for 'big', e.g. 'huge', and puts it in a different sentence.

Player 1 now chooses another alternative.

Play continues until one player gets stuck.

Re-match? Start with 'small' or choose your own descriptive word, such as 'happy'.

School extra

Consider the statement *'All children should remain at school until 4.00pm.'*

Think about and discuss

What might this mean to the children and their families? Would this be a good idea?

Ask for the opinion of others and consider your own views. What are the advantages and disadvantages?

Prepare a one-minute talk to present and explain your opinion. You will need some examples or evidence to help.

Once upon a time ...

Think through the main events of your day and begin to create an interesting story with imaginative additions.

- What did you do?
- Who was involved?
- Where did you go?
- How did you feel?

Think about these things as if they are part of a narrative and practise telling the 'story' of your day. Think about the order of events and be as detailed and descriptive as you can.

Tell someone the story and prepare a one-minute version to share at school.

Think about and discuss

How could you embellish the details and make even more imaginative additions?

whine

Broadcast genius

Aim of the activity

- To think about how speakers emphasise main points.

Watch the first ten minutes of a news broadcast on TV.

Tell someone at home what you noticed about it. Try and focus on how it was presented and how the news reader emphasised the main points. Did they use specific facial expressions, tone of voice, gestures and so on?

Think about and discuss

What would be your top three tips for excellent news reading?

How could you use your own tips to help you share information, e.g. in assemblies, in the future?

Share your tips with friends at school.

TV and radio signals

Aim of the activity

- To think about how language in broadcasts can be used to signal changes in focus.

 Ask someone at home to help you choose an informative programme on the TV or radio, e.g. *Natural World*.

Listen to/watch the broadcast together and then talk about what you have learned.

Think about and discuss

How did the broadcaster introduce new points? What kind of language was used? How did the broadcaster keep you engaged?

Think about expression and tone of voice. Were there any techniques you could copy in the future?

Create a one-minute broadcast of your own.

Media package

Aim of the activity

- To think about how music, words and pictures work together to make good TV.

Choose one of your favourite TV programmes.

Listen to the first three minutes, but do not watch the screen (you could be in a different room but still able to hear the TV).

Watch the next three minutes with the sound off.

Watch the last three minutes with the sound on.

Think about and discuss

How did you feel during each section and why?

Could you follow the story with sound but no pictures?

Could you follow the story with pictures but no sound?

Which were most important to the programme?

Chatterbox

Think about all of the words you would use to greet friends at school, e.g. 'hiya' or 'hello'. Now think about phrases for saying goodbye.

 Ask an adult to share all the words they would use to greet their work colleagues. Would their greetings change if they were meeting new people?

Compare the words – which are the same/different?

Think about and discuss

Which greetings would you use if you were meeting your headteacher, your friend, the Queen, a famous footballer or the postman?

Would these words be different if you asked your teacher, your grandparents or your neighbours? What words do your grandparents use that you don't?

Think about whether you have noticed any patterns.

Complex conversation

People interact in lots of different ways. Sometimes they use facial expressions instead of speech to communicate, and these expressions and gestures are very important.

Imagine that 'the cat has got your tongue' and that you cannot speak for ten minutes. (It might help to warn the people at home or at school.)

Watch how people around you communicate and respond to each other in their discussions. Listen to a conversation and do your best to 'take part', but remember that you cannot speak – what do you do?

Think about and discuss

What happens in a conversation when people talk to each other but do not look at each other's faces? What happens when speakers use gestures as well as speech?

Tell someone what you have learned about communication.

Artful argument

Aim of the activity

- To identify main points in arguments and compare how they are presented.

Try and persuade someone at home to do a chore that they would normally refuse, e.g. washing up, vacuuming, homework!

Listen carefully to their argument for not doing it.

Think about and discuss

What are their main points? How do you know that these are the key issues? How is their argument different to your own?

Discuss who you think is the most persuasive and consider why.

Find someone to hold a longer debate with and ask them to argue the opposing points. You will try to persuade them that you should not tidy your room. Think carefully about the points you want to make.

Speaking, listening and interacting

Sharing a good yarn

Ask someone at home to tell you their favourite story. It could be a well-known tale or a story about someone in the family.

What were the 'main points' of the tale?

Pick out the three most important bits and make some cue cards to help you remember them. You can use pictures or symbols on the cards to help you re-tell the story.

Share the story, using your cards to help you be as entertaining as you can. Can you repeat any of the really good bits to encourage the listeners to join in with the story?

Think about and discuss

Which of your prompt cards was the most useful and why? How might you use this technique again in the future?

Quirky questions

Aim of the activity

- To explore different types of question.

Write down the names of six different places, e.g. Australia, on some strips of paper.

Put the strips in a 'hat' and ask someone to pull one out.

Give them two minutes in which to think of as many questions as they can about that place. (Remember, you don't need to know the answers!)

Think about and discuss

What kinds of questions have they asked? Which ones would require the longest answers? Which ones can be answered and which cannot? How could you find out the answers?

Swap over, so that the other person is in charge of the hat, and put in six different animal names.

This time, you think of the questions, taking as long as you need to include some different question types.

What kind of questions did you ask?

Think about and discuss

Why do we need to be able to ask questions in different ways?

Cor, what a car!

Aim of the activity

- To present a persuasive argument.

Imagine that you could design and make your own dream car (or any other item). Draw and colour your design.

Present it to an audience, telling them how the design was conceived. Make sure you explain its 'special features'.

Can you persuade them that they should buy it?

 ## Think about and discuss

Which details are the most persuasive? How can you convince the audience that the car is everything they need?

Special occasion speech

 Ask an adult at home to tell you about their proudest moment. Listen very carefully to the words they use.

Ask them to tell you again, but this time they should stand up and imagine that they are in a hall with 100 strangers, making a speech about what they've done. Think about how the speech is different.

Tell them what you noticed and why you think this is the case.

How did they feel the second time around?

Think about and discuss

How would you tell the same story to your friend or the Queen?

Persuasive power

Choose an appealing advertisement from a magazine or newspaper. Ask if you can cut it out and then show it to someone at home.

Point out the most persuasive language and think about how effective it is. Why do you think it is persuasive? What is it that makes it stand out?

Talk about the advertisement together and consider what other persuasive words could be used in this advert.

Think about and discuss

What changes would you make to improve the advertisement?

Could you design an advert for a similar product that is even more appealing? What kind of language would you use?

Note perfect

Ask an adult to read this text to you. While they read, make quick mental notes about the most important bits.

> *Trees*
>
> *Human life is dependent on trees. They sustain the balance of our atmosphere and support our diverse ecosystems. Scientists understand the importance of trees but storytellers also know that trees are a very important part of our history. In ancient times, trees were symbols of great power and mystery, perhaps because some can live for hundreds of years.*
>
> *Trees have long been an essential source of building materials and fuel, and we still use lots of trees for these purposes today. The English oak, for example, is well known for its strength and beauty, but did you know that in 1805 it was also used to build the huge ships for the Battle of Trafalgar?*

Now swap over, so that this time you read the text.

Talk about the points you remember most and whether they are different or the same.

Think about and discuss

What do you need to listen out for when trying to remember details?

What do you need to know at the start to help make mental notes?

What will you remember about this kind of note-taking in the future?

Weather watch

Aim of the activity

- To consider how speakers present points using different words and gestures.

Watch a weather forecast on TV and think about how the presenter uses their voice and hands.

Try and remember some of the key phrases and particular 'weather' words.

Draw a weather map to be shared with someone at home and put it up somewhere so that you can stand in front of it.

Practise giving the weather forecast and ask the audience to give you marks out of ten for language and gesticulation!

Prepare to share a version of your forecast at school.

Decisions, decisions

Aim of the activity

- To understand the process of decision making.

Imagine that someone gave you a year's worth of pocket money in one go.
What would you decide to do with it and how would you decide?

 ## Think about and discuss

Is talking important when people are making decisions? Does talking make it easier or harder to make a choice?

Maximum moaning

Aim of the activity

- To understand how to criticise constructively.

Maximus 'the Moaner' criticises everything. Read each of his statements aloud to someone at home and try to sound as 'whingy' as possible.

> *'I told you that I hate jam sandwiches. They always taste soggy.'*
> *'Nobody likes this programme. It's boring.'*
> *'Why aren't we going swimming again today? You never let me go swimming when I want to.'*
> *'That story was rubbish. It didn't make sense.'*
> *'I want to sit in the front of the car. You should sit in the back.'*

Consider why these statements seem harsh and inappropriate. Which words or phrases make it impossible to sound positive and 'upbeat'?

Think about and discuss

Think about what you might change or add in order to make the criticism more constructive and helpful. Choose one of the statements above and make it more positive.

Now talk about your ideas with someone at home.

Drama, performance and presentation

Miming magic

Look at this list of ordinary household activities:

- teeth cleaning
- washing up
- ironing
- getting dressed
- making sandwiches.

Think about how you can mime each of these to someone at home and ask them to try and guess what you are doing.

When you've finished, ask them to think of their own activities and swap over.

Think about and discuss

Which mimes were the best and why?

What were the best 'clues' and actions?

How important are facial expressions in performing different mimes?

Knock, knock ... who's there?

Aim of the activity

- To present a character and engage an audience.

Think of a well-known fairytale and the different characters who appear in it. (Don't tell anyone what it is!)

Gather an audience if you can and tell them that when you knock on the door, they must invite you in so that you can introduce yourself.

Take on the role of one of the fairytale characters and tell them about yourself without mentioning your name.

Ask them to try and identify the fairytale that you belong to. If they are stuck, knock again and try another character until they guess correctly.

Think about and discuss

How well did you engage your audience? What did you need to do to keep them engaged?

Which were the most important character clues?

What was the most difficult part of trying to present your character?

How am I?

Aim of the activity

- To think about how different expressions can be interpreted in drama.

Ask someone at home to help you think of as many different emotions as you can, e.g. happy, angry, bored or frustrated.

Tell them that you are going to use facial expressions and behaviour to portray five of these feelings. You can use gestures and sound effects but cannot speak.

Ask them to try and identify which emotion you are portraying. Discuss which emotions were the hardest to portray and why.

Now swap over and ask them to demonstrate the behaviour and expressions associated with five other emotions. Can you identify them correctly?

Which emotions can be interpreted in more than one way?

Think about and discuss

How could you use these observations to help you create interesting characters in story writing?

The world's a stage

Aim of the activity

• To make up a scene using improvisation.

Use this prompt to start you off and ask someone to help you continue the dialogue. You'll need to think quickly and listen carefully to the lines spoken before your turn as you take it in turns to speak.

Try and continue the scene for at least six more turns and deliver your words with as much expression as possible.

> You: (very excitedly) You'll NEVER guess what I saw on my way home from school today!
> Them: Well, it must have been something pretty unusual. You're not usually this keen to share your news. Was it …?

When you've finished, discuss what skills you need to be able to improvise well and think about the ways in which you could improve in the future.

Picture this

Aim of the activity

- To use illustrations to enrich a story.

Think of a story that you know well and prepare to tell it to someone at home. It might be helpful to use a traditional tale that they know well too.

Ask them to comment on how you made the story flow and work with them to identify four main events in the story.

Draw a picture of each of these events, and/or the characters involved, on four small pieces of paper.

Use these drawings to help you tell the story again, this time adding as much detail as possible about the people, places and events involved.

Think about and discuss

How effective were your drawings for the purpose of prompting and enriching your story?

How did they help you to describe the people and events?

What did you like about your drawings and why?

Story maker

Did you know that authors often plan their stories around a central 'problem'? The story often ends when the problem has been resolved.

Imagine three characters to help form the basis of an adventure story: the hero/heroine, the 'baddy', and the hero/heroine's best friend.

Think about your ideas for a central problem and discuss them with someone at home.

Decide on an event, e.g. the baddy steals a precious item and the hero/heroine must return it.

Think about and discuss

How will the hero/heroine manage to accomplish his/her task?

What happens to the baddy at the end of the story?

Try to remember the beginning, middle and end of your story and be prepared to share your ideas at school.

Creating a character

Aim of the activity

- To describe interesting characters and engage interest.

Find a photo of a person (who you do not know) from a magazine or leaflet and keep it secret.

Use this photo to help you describe that person to someone at home, adding as much detail as you can, so that they can then draw them.

When they have finished drawing, compare their image with the photo that you used. How could you have refined your description to make the subject more interesting? What other details did you need to add?

Use the drawing to help you think about a short character description. This should focus on what the character is like, rather than how they appear. What sort of personality does this character have? Think about how you would describe them.

When you've had a chance to think about your character, give them a name and describe them to someone at home.

Ask them to comment on how well you engaged their interest with your character description.

Fact-finding mission

Aim of the activity

- To summarise and talk about material from different informative sources.

Choose a place, hobby, famous person or pet that you are particularly interested in and find out as much as you can about your chosen subject by looking at lots of different sources. You can use books, magazines, newspapers, the radio, TV, the internet and the people around you.

When you've thought about an appropriate order for 'key points', share all of the information you've found with someone at home and consider whether there is anything else that you'd like to know.

Think about and discuss

Why did you choose this topic? What did you learn about it?

What have you learned about your own 'fact-finding' skills?

Prepare a 30-second talk about your work to share with friends back at school.

Drama, performance and presentation

Thespian dreams

Aim of the activity

- To perform a scripted scene (soliloquy).

Read the script very carefully and pay attention to stage directions. You will need to be confident and perform this for someone at home using different voices, expressions and gestures.

Alas, I've had the toughest time of late,
                    (Pacing, head shaking, thoughtful expression)
Learning spellings, practising sums, writing stories to date.
                    (Counting off fingers, earnest look at audience)
Who would have thought that the challenge should be thus?
                    (Palms up, arms out, questioning expression)
And who is it that decides these tasks should fall on us?
                    (More head shaking, puzzled expression)
I can see from past experience that the secret to success
                    (Nodding, smile)
Is confidence, determination, knowledge more-or-less,
                    (Nodding continues, rubbing hands together,
                    more-or-less gesture with hand)
And yet it is a puzzle that to school we go each day
                    (Fingers gripping chin as if deep in thought)
When sometimes we could learn these things through toil outside and play.
                    (Sit down, more thinking, look at audience to convince them)
Still ... it soon will be much clearer how on this path I'll tread,
                    (Tap watch, stand up, nod, point to self, walk straight line)
I just wish sometimes that I'd missed school and stayed at home instead.
                    (Smile, chuckle, sit down again, nodding)

When the audience have finished clapping, ask them to give you feedback on what went well and why. Consider how you can use this advice in the future.

Wizard wonders

Aim of the activity

- To recognise the potential impact of 'effects' in drama.

Look at the passage below, which focuses on a wizard casting his spell, and consider what he's trying to do.

> *(The wizard stands behind a huge, black, metal cauldron and reads from a book as he begins to perform his spell)*
> *Into the pot I throw the weeds that make our time run backward,*
> *I add the powdered bone and wood and stir the water forward.*
> *If breakfast is to supper turn and daylight back to night,*
> *Then I will need a witch's skill and also giant's might.*
> *In goes the sulphur, soil and sand with cup of sugar sweet,*
> *Up rush the bubbles, swift and fast, as I stir in the heat.*
> *The day it fast begins to turn and night it soon will come,*
> *How strange it is to see the moon when day is yet to run.*
> *This spell, it reaches its sharp end and owls begin to call,*
> *The blanket of the dark is here and evening curtains fall.*

You are going to try and dramatise this scene, so think about how certain effects could enhance the drama. Discuss the potential impact of colours, costume, lighting, movement, props and sound effects and ask someone to help you create the scene.

Make the drama as exciting as possible and use your voice to give real character to the wizard. What impact do your chosen effects have on the atmosphere?

Playhouse

Aim of the activity

- To devise a performance for an audience at home.

Think of a well-known story (a fairytale, myth, fable or legend might be good) and consider all of the characters involved.

Choose two of these characters and make up a scene that involves them both in some kind of action or conversation. You will need to think about their role in the story (e.g. what do they do?) and what their personalities are like.

Find someone to play the second character while you take the lead role and practise improvising a scene until you're happy with it.

If possible, perform it for someone else and ask them to evaluate your work by considering what went well and why.

Think about and discuss

Do you agree with their comments or not?

How could your performance be improved?

What was the most challenging part?

Word art

Choose one of your favourite colours and close your eyes. Think about what that colour would taste and feel like. What would it sound and smell like? What does it look like to you?

Now find out as much factual information as you can about that colour. Where do you find it? How is it made? What is it commonly used for? You can use books, dictionaries, magazines and any other sources that are helpful.

Tell someone at home about your thoughts and the things that you've found out.

Think about and discuss

How could some of these ideas inspire a short piece of poetry? It could be very simple like the one below.

What is purple?

Purple is a quiet rush of juicy, velvet pudding
Purple is the heavy sound of rich, dark berries ripening
Purple is my favourite pastille … chewy, sugary, sweet.

Now try and improvise a verse together entitled 'What is black/red/yellow…?' or whatever colour you chose. (Tip! Your spoken verse does not have to rhyme!)

Enhanced reporting

Aim of the activity

- To vary pace and develop detail when presenting information.

Choose a news story on the radio or TV that captures your imagination in some way. Think about the style of the language used.

Use the story as a prompt for telling your own news story, which can be as imaginary as you wish to make it as exciting as possible.

Think about and discuss

How can you share your story and practise telling it to someone at home? Consider the pace and level of detail and make your 'news-casting voice' as convincing as possible.

Why is detail important in news stories? What can a change of pace do?

Think of three 'top tips' for good reporting.

Storyteller

Aim of the activity

- To use different narrative techniques to engage and entertain the audience.

Choose a favourite myth, fable or legend (e.g. Theseus and the Minotaur, The Hare and the Tortoise, King Arthur) and practise telling the story in front of a mirror.

Make the story as scary, funny or mysterious as possible by using different voices, vocabulary and facial expressions.

Think about what different narrative techniques you can use, e.g. pauses, loud voices, gesticulation and so on.

 Tell someone at home the story and ask them to comment on which techniques were the most engaging.

Prepare a one-minute version of your story to share at school.

Spooky work

Ask someone at home to tell you a ghost story that they know well or were told as a child.

Try and remember the main points and ask them to help you find some music that might go with the story.

Draw four pictures of the main parts of the narrative and ask them to help you practise telling the story yourself.

Now gather an audience (if you can) and use your pictures, and the music, to make your storytelling particularly spooky. If you can't find any music, sound effects will do, but make sure it's quite dark!

Afterwards, ask the audience to tell you what they thought of your performance and think about which bits you enjoyed the most.

Reading and responding

First choices

Aim of the activity

- To share and compare reasons for reading preferences.

Ask someone at home what they most like to read. Do they prefer novels and stories, or newspapers and magazines? Why do they think this is?

Consider what your favourite and least favourite book is. Why did you enjoy it, or dislike it, so much?

Think about and discuss

What kind of texts do you read most often? What do you find appealing?

Read the two limericks below and choose your favourite. Think about why you like this one best and prepare to share your ideas back at school.

> *There was a young girl on a trike,*
> *Who said that she really did like*
> *A trip through the park*
> *Between sunset and dark*
> *To practise for riding a bike.*

> *There was an old man in a hat,*
> *Who said it was simple as that,*
> *To look very smart*
> *In a barrow or cart*
> *Providing cross-legged you sat.*

Dealing with a dilemma

Aim of the activity

- To empathise with characters and consider dilemmas.

Read and discuss the extract below with someone at home.

Think about how the characters feel and why.

Our little bear was trapped in the cage as the scientists sat around the fire discussing their research. They seemed to think that studying this species would help them to understand what was wrong with the other creatures in the forest but my brother and I were both really worried that our little bear cub would not be treated well. We didn't want all of the forest animals to go on suffering but how did anyone know that looking at the bear cub might actually be the same as everything else. It seemed stupid to think that experimenting on him could help them understand what was happening to the squirrels and birds and fish. We snuck up to the cage and pulled hard on the lock but the metal was old and rusty and squeaked when we turned it. We both knew that letting the bear out was very risky but we didn't want him to be treated like some kind of lab rat. 'These tests could mean the difference between life and death for this whole ecosystem', one of the men said, 'and it would be wonderful to bring new life back to this area.' We looked at each other and hesitated. My brother seemed really concerned. 'Are we doing the right thing?' he whispered. I looked at him and shrugged.

Think about and discuss

What would you do if faced with this dilemma? Would you put one creature at risk in order to help others?

Talk about your ideas. Can you think of a possible solution?

Why write?

Aim of the activity

- To explore how and why authors write.

Think of your favourite author and consider why he/she might want to write. Have a look at the blurb on one of their books and see if this gives you any clues. Brainstorm ideas and share with someone else.

Think about and discuss

Why do you like their writing so much?

Is there anything distinctive about their writing?

If you can, search for material on the internet (with someone at home or at school) which reveals how and why your author writes.

Share your findings at school.

Point spotting

Read the extract below and consider the main points.

Looking after your hamster

Hamsters make very good pets for young children. They are easy to look after and are relatively clean and tidy! Young hamsters are very easy to tame and can be stroked and petted often. They live in desert regions in the wild and like to dig and make tunnels for themselves. There are lots of different kinds of hamster cages, but solid-based containers are better for their feet. Hamsters like to climb and will chew on pieces of wood and cardboard, which is good because their teeth are always growing. There are many different kinds of hamster but most need to live by themselves. They eat seeds, nuts and fruit and enjoy the occasional treat. They are often very friendly and can live for two to three years.

Key equipment	Daily care routine	Top tips
Hamster cage or tank Sawdust and soft bedding Water bottle Food bowl Tube or tunnel Nest box Material for gnawing	Change the water and top up the food bowl Offer a very small amount of fresh food, e.g. a grape Allow your hamster to exercise outside the cage/tank every day, but never leave him/her alone. Adventurous hamsters can disappear under floorboards!	Make sure that you clean your hamster's cage/tank out every week. Soiled bedding can become very smelly!

Active facts

Roborovski hamsters are very small and can be kept in pairs. They have beautiful coloured patterns in their coats and are sometimes smaller than 9 cm. Syrian hamsters are much bigger and must live alone. They come in lots of different colours and sometimes have long hair that needs brushing occasionally.

Think about and discuss

What kind of text is this? How do you know?

Ask someone else to read the extract and then share your summary of the main points with them. Do they agree that these are the key points?

Text reviewer

Think about and discuss

How many different text types can you find at home? You can include books, the TV and internet if you wish, as well as magazines, reference texts, leaflets and so on.

Choose three different texts and think about how the words and pictures are organised. Think about their style and appearance, as well as the content of the text.

Decide how each of the texts is similar or different to the others and think of examples that you can share at school, e.g. consider their key features.

Discuss why you think these texts are organised differently.

Use the clues

Ask someone to listen to you read the extract below. This is from a story called 'Sunshine and Catfish'.

> *Polly had been sitting on the bench for ages but Kate still hadn't come. The others were waiting by the rock-pool as agreed but Polly was beginning to think that something had gone wrong. They had given Kate the right time and she could easily catch the usual bus from her grandma's so why was she so late? Why hadn't she turned up smiling ages ago? She was so looking forward to a day at the beach. Polly was just thinking about how she could get a message to the others when a car pulled up. It wasn't one that Polly recognised so she moved away from the kerb.*

Think about the character of Polly and discuss with your partner how you think she is feeling. You need to be able to say why you think this and use the text to support your ideas.

Think about and discuss

What do they think will happen next?

Can they use the text to justify their ideas?

Do you agree with them?

Explain what you think will happen next and say why by referring to the story.

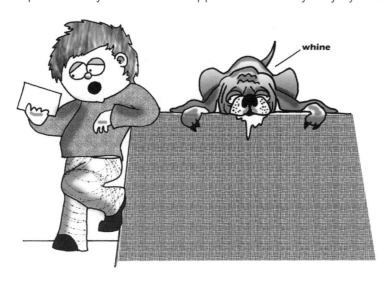

whine

Picture perfect

Aim of the activity

- To consider how writers use language to create images and atmosphere.

Read this extract carefully and think about how it makes you feel and why.

> *The small boy stepped out of the ragged hole. No one knew he was there or how long he'd been awake, watching, wondering, waiting. He already knew that the villagers were hungry and that their animals had long since run away. The road to the town was purple in the moonlight and the trees were coal black at the edge of every ditch. He moved quietly through the shadows, his gaze focused on the windows of the darkest little cottage which cowered just outside the village walls.*

Now read the extract again to someone at home and discuss which are the most powerful lines and why.

Think about and discuss

What do you imagine as you read the text? What pictures can you see in your head?

How has the writer used language to create images and atmosphere? Which words are really important and what effect do they have on you?

Discuss which parts of the extract you would edit and why. Can you change the atmosphere and imagery by changing the words used?

Reading and responding

Reflecting on reading

Aim of the activity

- To reflect on personal reading habits and preferences and set reading goals.

Talk about your feelings towards reading with someone at home.

When is the best time to read? What do you like to read?

How do your reading preferences compare with theirs?

Think about and discuss

What kind of reading goals could you set for each other, to be achieved by the end of the week? For example, you might want to read more fluently, with more expression or just more frequently.

Whatever your goals are, consider how you might achieve them.

A happy theme

Think about what it means to be happy to you. What are your favourite things? What makes you smile?

Now think about how the theme of happiness can be presented in writing by reading the texts below.

Happiness is...
A picnic in the summer,
A rainbow after rain,
A purr from your lap,
A blackbird's chorus,
An ice cream in Italy,
A pile of leaves to pounce in,
A bouncy castle,
A baby's giggle,
A strawberry jelly,
A warm memory,
An impending birthday,
A smile.

She shouted at me that I was too 'happy-go-lucky', though I wasn't convinced that she knew what it meant. I stomped off to my house and looked the phrase up in a dictionary. It said 'cheerfully casual' which sounded good to me. The dictionary also said 'Happy medium – a compromise; Happy event – a birth, and Happy hunting ground – a place of success'. I wrote down the bit about 'happy medium' and thought about how I'd get her to change her mind. It was my turn to pick the next project after all and I wanted this one to be brilliant.

Think about and discuss

Which portrayals of happiness are the most powerful?

Why do you think that this is the case?

Which text do you like best and why?

Book review

Aim of the activity

* To read extensively and discuss personal reading with others.

Finish reading a really good book and prepare to present a book review to a group of classmates.

Consider a summary of your chosen text and explain how you responded to the text and why.

Practise sharing your book review (as a presentation) at home.

Think about and discuss

What would persuade your friends to read this book?

What did you particularly like about it?

A really good read

Choose a book or novel that you think will challenge you and read it regularly to someone at home.

Ask them to think about how you make the text 'come alive' when you are reading to them and if they can suggest any other ways.

Listen to them reading to you and consider how they make the text engaging.

Think about and discuss

What techniques do you both use to make the text more interesting?

Have you learned any new techniques that you will use in the future?

Possible perspectives

Read the character description below to someone at home and consider whether or not you think the writer likes the character.

This woman was not a good-natured person and her devious thoughts often showed on her face. Her eyes, which were hooded by heavy, wrinkled lids, always seemed to be dark and lifeless. She never smiled but, instead, often smirked at those around her, especially small children whose presence made her anxious, irritable and annoyed. Today, she seemed even more agitated than usual as she sat, with hands shaking, in a brown velvet chair. She peered down into the street, like a crow looking for carrion, and laughed to herself as she remembered what she'd done.

Think about and discuss

Which part of the text seems to be the biggest clue about the writer's feelings? Which words or phrases suggest how the writer feels?

How do you feel about this character? How has the writer tried to influence you?

What do you think is implied by the first and last lines of the text? Prepare to share your ideas at school.

Tickle your funny bone?

Aim of the activity

- To explore how writers use language for comic and dramatic effects.

Practise reading this extract to someone at home.

Podsbill stood up and shook the itching powder out of his vest while Sampson rolled around in the ditch, clutching his stomach and howling with laughter. 'It's not funny you know,' grumped Podsbill, as he tried to rearrange his vest and stuff it back into his trousers. 'We were already late for the party and now we'll probably miss out on the apple bobbing and jelly.' Sampson got to his feet and tried to look suitably sorry but every time he caught a glimpse of Podsbill trying to scratch his back on the bark of a willow tree, he couldn't help but collapse into another fit of giggles. 'Come on,' grumbled Podsbill as he steered Sampson on by his collar. 'We'll get there for tea if you walk a bit quick....,' but he fell over his laces before he could finish and ended up spluttering in a well-placed puddle. Sampson went back to clutching his stomach and shrieking as before, while Podsbill scowled ... 'very funny.'

Read it again, making it as comical as possible.

Think about and discuss

Which parts of the extract influence the way you read it? Why did you read it the way you did?

Which parts of the extract are particularly dramatic? What could you add to make it better still?

Share your ideas about the language used and explain them to someone else.

Paper clipping

Find a recent newspaper story that interests you. Check with an adult that it is an appropriate choice.

Read the headline and consider what questions you might have about that topic. What would you expect the story to tell you?

Scan the text and think about what you have found out. Has it answered all of the questions that you had, or is there anything missing?

 ## Think about and discuss

How useful is this text in finding out about the topic? Explain why you think this by referring to the newspaper story.

The tale of the tail

Read extract one to someone at home and consider what this well-known tale might be. How do you know? Who is telling this story?

Extract one

If he hadn't been about to eat the girl, I wouldn't have done it, but what choice did I have? It was either swing the axe and damage him or just stand by and watch as he polished her off. I was sure he'd already made a meal of grandma. A wolf can live without his tail anyway, so I don't think we should be too worried about him. The little girl went home to her mother although we never did find her cape. I can't imagine she'll go walking through those woods again.

Now read extract two and consider how it compares to the first. This is based on the same tale but how is this version different? Whose point of view is this?

Extract two

I was just leaning across to pick up the basket when that man burst in and started yelling and swiping at me with his chopper. I was really shocked. It was all so unnecessary. I tried to reason with him but he seemed surprised that I was capable of speaking and didn't understand that Red and I are friends. I would never have done anything to harm her. Who else am I going to play hide and seek in the woods with? Now, I've got no tail and the other wolves have laughed at me. They think I'm a wimp just because I get nervous when I have to go off the path for more firewood.

'Both extracts have been written by different characters in the story.'

What evidence is there that this statement is true?

Can you think of any other characters who might give a different version? Tell someone at home.

Spelling, punctuation and structure

Spelling ace

You need two players, some paper, a pen and scissors. An adult would be helpful to adjudicate!

Cut some paper into 26 similar pieces – one for each letter of the alphabet.

Write each letter on one of the pieces and then make separate groups for the vowels and the consonants.

Turn each piece face down and decide who goes first.

Player 1 selects six pieces, including one or two vowels, and turns them over to display the letters.

Player 1 must make a word using each letter as desired. (Tip – they can miss some letters out or use them more than once if they want to!)

One point is awarded for each letter they have used in a correct spelling. There are two extra points if they can put the word in a sentence.

Swap over. The first player to 20 points wins.

Word wall

This is a game about spelling and tactics! You need two players and a pen to record your results on the word wall below. An adult would be helpful to adjudicate!

Column 1 is for words of one letter. Column 2 is for words with two letters. Column 3 is for words with 3 letters and so on. The foundations of the wall have already been laid. You need to build on the X at the bottom of each column.

1 LETTER	2 LETTERS	3 LETTERS	4 LETTERS	5 LETTERS
Start here				
X				
X	Start here			
X	X			
X	X	Start here		
X	X	X		
X	X	X	Start here	
X	X	X	X	
X	X	X	X	Start here

Decide who is going first and ask them to choose a column. They will need to consider tactics because ten points are awarded to the player who completes the last brick in the column. No points are awarded for individual bricks.

Player 1 should spell out any word they like, *as long as it has the correct number of letters*, and claim the next brick in the column by adding their initials if their spelling was correct.

Player 2 then chooses a column and repeats the exercise. They should aim to claim the next brick by adding their initials.

The game continues, with players taking turns to choose a column and spell out a word, until all of the bricks are filled.

Remember that spellings must be correct and the highest scorer wins the game.

Spelling rules

Ask an adult at home if they can remember any spelling rules from school, e.g. 'i before e except after c' (receive), 'big elephants can always understand small elephants' (because), 'one collar two socks' (necessary).

Now think of a word that you find difficult to spell and ask them to help you think of a rule or a mnemonic

Practise using the rule to see if it works and remember to share it with friends.

Are there any other rules that you can remember?

"i" before "e" except after "c"

Try and invent mnemonics for the following:

Rhythm, e.g. rhythm helps your two hips move
Separate
Recommend
Beautiful
Friend
Definitely
Autumn

Try and use your mnemonics to help you in the future.

Be a wordsmith

Aim of the activity

- To think about interesting word roots and how they can influence spelling.

Correct spelling can be quite tricky because English has evolved from many different languages. Words which end in 'i', for example, are often borrowed from Italian.

❓ **Ask someone** at home to help you think of as many words as you can which end in 'i'.

Discuss what you notice about them. What do they often refer to? What do they mean?

Can you think of any other words that we've borrowed from a different language, e.g. 'prayer' from French.

Have a look in a dictionary for some of your favourite words and see if you can spot where they come from. (Tip – the notes at the front of dictionaries often help!)

Sentence maker

Aim of the activity

- To compose precise sentences using adjectives, verbs and nouns.

Tell someone at home what you think an adjective, a verb and a noun is.

How many examples of these can you think of together?

Now make up a sentence about what you did at school and ask someone else to listen out for nouns, verbs and adjectives.

Did your sentence have a noun, verb and an adjective in it?

Try another sentence – is it the same?

Think about and discuss

Which words do you need most to help the sentence make sense? Are they nouns, verbs or adjectives? Can you miss any of these words out?

Tell someone what you have noticed.

Coping with clauses

Ask someone at home to help you with this. You'll need a pair of scissors.

A subordinate clause adds detail to the main part of a sentence but is not essential to help the sentence make sense. For example, 'Dad came back from the shop and sat down to watch TV' could become 'Dad came back from the shop, before the football started, and sat down to watch TV' with a subordinate clause.

Cut the sentences below into strips and put them in a hat. Decide who is going first with the following task.

Take it in turns to select a strip and read the sentence aloud. You must then read the sentence again but, this time, adding a subordinate clause. Keep the strip if you manage it successfully but give it to your partner if you don't.

The winner is the person who has collected the most sentence strips.

The cat jumped onto the floor.

Mum tried to clean up the mess before anyone saw it.

My sister scored two goals today.

The clouds looked like clumps of cotton wool.

We are going to visit our grandparents at the weekend.

Kathy ran up to the fence as quickly as she could.

Everyone ran towards the beach because the weather was really hot and they wanted to sit in the sun.

Most people found that the pudding was too sour because the fruit wasn't really ripe.

Unscramble the jumble

Aim of the activity

- To clarify meaning and point of view by exploring sentence structure.

Look very closely at the long sentence below and try to 'unpick' the main parts by reading it aloud.

> *Billy thought that James was being very unfair and hadn't considered the feelings of all the other kids who were also anxious about the lack of progress with their new ice cream flavours and the fact it wasn't their fault that the cream had curdled, the sugar had burnt and the mixture wouldn't set.*

Discuss with someone at home how many different points appear in this sentence.

Think about what you could do to improve the structure of the text and make the sentence easier to read.

What have you learned about clarity?

's or s'?

An apostrophe can be used to help show possession, i.e. who owns what. We can use a 'belonging to' phrase to help us remember where to put the apostrophe (e.g. *the socks belonging to James* becomes *James' socks*) because the apostrophe always goes after the name.

Look at this list of boys' names and think of six different objects that they could own.

> *James; Sam; Ben; Nicholas; Jack; Peter*

Match each name to an object and talk about the placement of each apostrophe.

Do this again with the six girls' names below (e.g. the pen belonging to Samantha = Samantha's pen).

> *Jess; Alice; Rachel; Laura; Lucy; Alexis*

Think about and discuss

What do you notice about the names which have an 's' at the end, e.g. James and Jess? Where do you put the apostrophe?

What do you notice about the names that do not end in 's', e.g. Sam?

How can you remember where to put the apostrophe? What is the rule where names end in 's'?

Pondering paragraphs

Read the text below, paying attention to the paragraphs, and then discuss these questions: Why has the writer used paragraphs? What do they do and where do they go?

Council Offices,
District of Whizby-on-Avon

Mr A. Man
123 Appleton Drive
Whizby-on-Avon
Appleshire

Dear Mr Man,

I regret to inform you that your recent application for a new skateboard ramp has been unsuccessful. At our last meeting all members of the council agreed that a new ramp in your back garden would be wholly inappropriate and that there would not be room for a ramp of this size.

I understand that you feel your children would benefit greatly from the additional exercise but we also have concerns on health and safety grounds.

If you would like to reconsider the size and scale of the ramp and could seek advice about how your project can be completed safely, please advise us by return post.

Yours sincerely,
A. Squiggle
Local Councillor

Ask an adult how they were taught to use paragraphs and what they use them for. Think about how you can remember to use them in your own writing.

Add an adverb, connect a conjunction

 Tell someone at home what you think adverbs and conjunctions are. Try to give them examples, e.g. 'quickly' is an adverb, 'and' is a conjunction.

Think about how you can change this sentence by adding an adverb and changing the conjunction.

> *Phillip walked down the road and turned into the lane.*

 Can you make it more interesting? **Tell someone** your new sentence.

Can you make the sentence longer? Share your ideas.

 ## Think about and discuss

What is the longest sentence you can make with this by playing with adverbs and conjunctions?

Take it in turns to add extra detail and see where Phillip ends up!

Spelling, punctuation and structure

Fixing words

Aim of the activity

- To practise using prefixes and suffixes accurately.

A prefix is an addition to the beginning of a word that can change the word's meaning, e.g. satisfactory becomes unsatisfactory with the prefix 'un'. A suffix is added to the end of a word and can also change meaning, e.g. eat becomes eating with the suffix 'ing'.

You will need a partner.

Take it in turns to think of a word with the prefix 'im', e.g. impossible, and keep going for as long as you can.

Who suggested the most words? How did they think of them?

Do the exercise again with the prefix 'un', e.g. unfit. Count how many words you suggest and explain your strategy.

Can anyone think of a word with the suffix 'ian', e.g. magician? What does the word mean? Can you suggest others?

Think about and discuss

What do you notice about the 'ian' words?

Herding words

? **Ask someone** who reads a lot to help you brainstorm as many 'ough' words as possible.

Think about and discuss

Which is the most unusual 'ough' word and what does it mean?

Are there any other 'ough' words that share the same sounds?

How many different sounds can 'ough' make?

What do you notice about the groups of words, their sounds or their meanings?

Trumping the tricky ones

Aim of the activity

* To spell difficult words using helpful strategies.

'Onomatopoeia' can be very difficult to spell. Tell someone at home what it means and teach them to spell it. Think about ways you can help them remember. Can you make up a rule or mnemonic to help?

Many adults find it hard to spell parallel, humorous, liaison and accommodation. Ask an adult to write these words down and explain how they try to remember the spelling.

Think about and discuss

Talk about which words they usually find difficult and compare these with yours.

Work together and find ways of remembering the correct spellings.

What have you learned that you can use in the future?

Signing sentences

Checking for punctuation can be dull, but sentences without it aren't really sentences! For this task, you need to develop a system of sentence 'sign language'.

Make up a set of symbols for capital letters, full-stops, commas, exclamation marks and question marks. Each symbol should be a shape that you can make with your fingers and hands.

Listen carefully to someone who is speaking slowly and try to punctuate their sentences using your signs. When you speak, you should also punctuate your own.

Can your partner suggest symbols for speech marks and apostrophes? Can you use them to punctuate a sentence?

Sounds like a sentence

Aim of the activity

- To punctuate sentences accurately, including speech marks and apostrophes.

Brainstorm as many different types of punctuation as you can.

Make up a sound symbol for each type, e.g. 1 clap = a full-stop, 1 table tap = a comma. Remember or note down the system.

Find someone to try and decode your sound effects (which you can make with your voice as well) by listening to some punctuated sentences. You will need to start with simple examples and practise punctuating them with your sounds before you share.

Encourage them to guess what your sound symbols mean.

Do they think that you are punctuating accurately?

Punctuation problem

Aim of the activity

- To use punctuation to clarify meaning.

Look at the short verses below and consider what difference the punctuation makes.

Verse 1

Tom says 'Roses are red,
And Violets are blue',
But which pairs of socks,
Belong to these two?

Verse 2

Tom says 'Rose's are red,
And Violet's are blue',
But which pairs of socks,
Belong to these two?

Discuss what you have noticed.

Think about and discuss

Why is it important to punctuate correctly? Think about its impact on both reading and writing.

whine

Scissor happy

Aim of the activity

- To experiment with the order of sections to achieve different effects.

Find an old newspaper or magazine and ask someone at home if you can cut it up.

Choose a story or article and have a look at the paragraphs, thinking about where they are used and why.

Take a pair of scissors and cut the story/article into separate sections, using the paragraphs to help you.

Lay out the pieces on a table and then begin to move the first and last sections around.

Play with the text until you have moved all of the pieces.

Think about and discuss

How does altering the order of the sections change the emphasis of the text? Is it more difficult or easier to read?

Consider how you might use this 'cutting' technique to help draft your own writing in the future.

What a pickle!

Read the recipe for 'pickled teacher jam' below and consider why the order does not make any sense.

- *Grate a carrot into the mixture and then add the pineapple and strawberry bootlaces*
- *Pickle a teacher in a large, air-tight jar with vinegar and fruit as described*
- *Tip the apricots and grapes into the cauldron and stir with a large twig*
- *Ingredients: one primary teacher – pickled in sweet balsamic vinegar with red cherries; one handful of dried apricots and one scoop of green grapes; three cups of runny honey and one cup of brown sugar*
- *Wait for one month until the flavours have combined and then drain the jar*
- *One tin of pineapple slices, three strawberry bootlaces and one grated carrot*
- *Two jugs of rain water*
- *Half a cup of beetroot juice and one spoon of piccalilli*
- *Chocolate sprinkles to add texture*
- *The honey and sugar should sweeten the mixture while the beetroot juice and piccalilli should add colour and 'bite'*
- *Save the teacher and the cherries*
- *When the mixture has reached bubbling point, stop stirring and allow to cool*
- *Add chocolate sprinkles before tipping into jam jars and selling at the school fayre*
- *Find a large cauldron and warm slowly before adding all of the rain water*

Use a pair of scissors to cut out each instruction and place the pieces on a table. Play with the order of the instructions until the text is more coherent.

Share your new text with someone at home and check that they can follow it easily.

Think about and discuss

How did you manage to re-order the instructions? Explain which 'key words' were really necessary to give the text shape.